Dream